TRACK AND SEARCH:
A DOG TRAINING GUIDE

David L Porter-MacDaibhéid

TRACK AND SEARCH: A DOG TRAINING GUIDE

© 2018 David Leslie Porter-MacDaibheid

David Leslie Porter-MacDaibheid has asserted his right under the Copyright, Design and Patents Act 1988 to be identified as the author of this work.

All rights reserved. No part of this publication may be reproduced, stored in a retrieval system, or transmitted, in any form, or by any means, electronic, mechanical, photocopying, recording or otherwise without prior permission of the copyright owner.

Paperback ISBN 978-0-9532221-9-3

Published by D L Porter-MacDaibheid

TRACK AND SEARCH: A DOG TRAINING GUIDE

To my son, Douglas (Dougie) Killick
(May 1991 – July 2021)

TABLE OF CONTENTS

INTRODUCTION

***

TRACKING AND EQUIPMENT

GRASS-SURFACE TRAINING

FIRST LESSON

STEP-BY-STEP DIAGRAMMATIC GUIDE

HARD-SURFACE TRACKING

LAYING TRACKS

THE SQUARE SEARCH

SQUARE SEARCH TRAINING

PRACTICAL APPLICATION

TRACK AND SEARCH: A DOG TRAINING GUIDE

INTRODUCTION

Why train a dog to track or to search?

Because it is fun. And anyway, apart from the enjoyment gained by both the handler and the dog, and along with the additional challenge of them being able to take part in Working Trial competitions where qualifications can be earned, there is a practical aspect to the exercise. A trained dog and handler team will have the ability to assist in the locating of vulnerable missing persons.

Imagine the scene. It is five o'clock on a cold, damp autumnal morning and you are abruptly woken by frenetic calls and an incessant banging at your front door. It is your elderly neighbour.

She is frantic with worry.

Her husband, who has for some time been showing the worsening signs of memory loss and with it, severe bouts of confusion, has, overnight, disappeared from their home.

She had woken to find that he was not beside her. On checking the kitchen, she had found the back door to be wide open. She had also been quick to notice that, with the dampness of the early morning mist having long replaced the warmth of the night-store heaters, the house had become cooled to such an extent that its internal temperature closely echoed that of the outside.

She knows that he can only be dressed in his pyjamas. His outdoor clothing is in the bedroom and his coat is still hanging in its usual place on a hook behind the kitchen door.

With the evidence of the chill having staked its claim throughout the house, it is acutely obvious that he has been gone for some time, and what with it being just a few degrees above freezing, he is particularly vulnerable.

There is no time to waste. He needs to be found. After all, he may well have become disorientated and, if he is not found soon, then he could easily succumb to the ravages of hypothermia.

You check the house and its precincts.

There is no sign of him.

You call out across the moors and listen for a reply.

There is none.

The police have the means to instigate a search, and so, on behalf of your neighbor, you make the call.

You have grave concerns for her husband's welfare, but you can do nothing other than to offer her some moral support whilst you both await the arrival of the local police officers.

It is likely that their arrival will be far from being instant as they have a large area to cover. What is more, with the usual reduction in staffing levels for a nightshift it is probable that those who are on duty will be patrolling the areas with the largest population. The truth is, they may need to travel many miles before they arrive at the doorstep.

Time is ticking by and, with each minute passing, there is the very real fear that by the time they arrive and take the relevant details, then gather their resources in order to make a search, it could already be too late.

The house backs on to a wilderness of gorse and heather-clad moors, which, being scarred with treacherous gullies and the roaring waters of hillside streams, is a landscape fraught with danger.

But what if the missing person is more fortunate than most? What if he has a neighbour with the means to instigate a search of their own and without necessarily having to await the arrival of the police?

If *you* are that neighbour with a dog who has been trained to track, then perhaps you can be proactive and commence a search without losing valuable time. By doing so you will waste no more time and may even prevent a tragedy!

TRACK AND SEARCH: A DOG TRAINING GUIDE

You keep calm and dress up warm. As you pick up the harness, your dog knows immediately what is in store. For him it is not a chore but rather it is a welcome opportunity, albeit unscheduled, for him to have some fun. This is the game where he is allowed to use his inherent abilities to track the scent of a person and, when the task has been successfully completed, he knows he will be rewarded with praise. After all, he is a dog, and although the ability to use his amazing sense of smell is just a natural part of his make-up, the fact is that it pleases his human companion when they work together and that is reward enough.

You and your dog stand at the open doorway and look out and across the wilderness. You are not ready to fit the harness quite yet, for you need to assess the situation first. You are looking for a marker, be it tangible, like footprints in the grass, or be it simply the most commonsense route for him to have taken.

You see the signs.

The dark imprint of footsteps having crushed the grass are still visible, heading out and in the direction of the heather and gorse-covered hillside.

Once he has left the grass and stepped into the heather, his trail will no longer be visible, but for the dog it is different — the scent will be as clear as day.

You slip the harness over the dog's head and calmly secure the buckles. Only then is the tracking-line clipped onto the metal ring which is fixed on the harness's back support.

Now it's over to him, the one with a natural ability to hunt well and truly rooted within his genes. You feel the pull on the line as he picks up the trail. You let out more line and then follow. He leads you for maybe a mile or so, across the rugged landscape.

Suddenly the pull on the line is strong. You are led to your confused and distraught neighbour who, shivering with the effects of the cold and damp, is huddled tightly in a ball and hidden within the shelter of the gorse.

He is alive, but only just! He has sprained his ankle and cannot walk. All you can do is keep him warm and use your mobile phone to call for assistance. You are a long way from a road, but at least you are there and are able to keep him safe whilst an air ambulance is summoned.

The police have only just arrived at the house but, thanks to the fact that your dog has been trained to track and you have had the wherewithal to make use of the skills, your neighbour has already been found and the appropriate rescue services are in the air.

Yes, this may well be no more than a piece of fiction, but it does serve to show how useful this form of training can be if ever the need arises. Perhaps it is not unlike training in the skills of first aid or resuscitation, in that it is good to know how to do it but hopefully you will not come across anyone who is in such a state of pain or distress that your skills are to be required.

In the following sections I have produced a relatively easy to understand, step-by-step guide from which I believe even the complete novice can successfully train a dog to track.

TRACKING AND EQUIPMENT

With the dog's sense of smell to the fore and whilst it is being controlled on a harness and line, the purpose of this exercise is for a dog and handler team to be able to follow the track (or trail) of a person, whether he, or she, is a stranger, or otherwise.

Practical tracks are run over a variety of ground surfaces. A dog and handler team will often seek to find a track several hours after the occurrence of an incident. Missing persons are rarely reported to the police immediately, and because of this, several hours may have elapsed before the commission of a crime, such as a burglary, becomes known.

This is why the track for a dog to negotiate in Working Trial Tracking Dog stakes must be a minimum of 3 hours old.

Whilst on the track, the dog should be trained to indicate to the handler the presence of any articles which possess the sought person's scent. In practical circumstances the article could well lead to the identification of the stranger if he, or she, is not located in person. For example, the article could well possess a fingerprint or, for that matter, a trace of DNA.

The line used to control the dog whilst tracking should be at least thirty feet long and is normally made from a soft cord such as sash-window cord or webbing. It is worth considering that some man-made fibres can, in certain circumstances, cause discomfort and burn marks to the handler's hands as the line suddenly pulls through them. I personally prefer the use of sash-window cord.

Most tracking-lines have a loop with a sixteen-inch circumference, or thereabouts, at each end. This makes it easy to fit a G-clip fastening at one end of the line, and the loop at the other can then be used as a handgrip. This loop prevents the line from slipping the handlers grasp in the event of the full length being in use.

The harness to be used for this exercise is normally manufactured from leather or webbing and should be designed so as to allow the dog to be comfortable and free to work without hindrance.

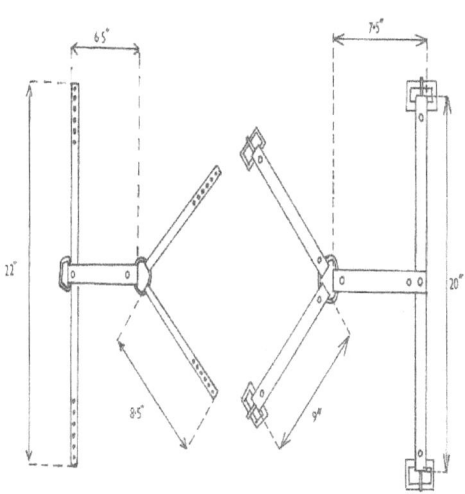

If unable to purchase a suitable harness, then a good saddler should be able to make one up from the above diagram. The measurements shown are suitable for a medium-size German Shepherd dog. The saddler should also be able to advise on the care and treatment of the harness and thereby prolong its working life.

For training purposes, and with regard to both tracking and searching, marker posts will be required to indicate the start of a training track, and also to indicate the corners of the square in the search.

The posts should be easily identifiable from a distance. They should therefore be of a bright colour and about three feet in length. They should be adapted so that they can be pushed into either hard or soft ground. I would suggest a length of bamboo cane, painted white, and with a six-inch nail secured in the bottom end. For the purposes of hard-surface tracking, such as tarmac or compacted earth, a post with a flat-bottomed surface, or even a small traffic cone would be ideal.

In United Kingdom Working Trials competitions, the end of the track is indicated by an article left by the tracklayer. The number of articles left between the starting post and the end article is dependent on the level of the working trials stake.

TRACK AND SEARCH: A DOG TRAINING GUIDE

In the first three tracking stakes, Utility Dog, Working Dog and Patrol Dog, there are two articles, including the end-of-track article. In the Tracking Dog stake there is an additional third.

It is advisable to have an article bag which contains a varied selection of items which are suitable to test the dog's ability to identify anything which possesses the strangers scent. These articles can be almost anything, so long as they are not injurious to the dog. Suitable articles could include shotgun, or 303, cartridge cases; three to six-inch lengths of cord, flex, card, plastic, carpet, lino etc.; bottle tops; key rings; corks; strips of leather and many others.

In addition to the aforementioned articles it is always worth carrying an article which the dog really enjoys playing with. A rubber bone, a rubber ring or a toddler's leather shoe are good examples.

Although many people use a hard rubber ball as a dog's plaything, I personally do not believe it to be the best of toys for a dog to play with.

It has been known for a dog to have started to choke having had a ball lodged in its throat. Then, with the saliva on the hardened rubber making its surface extremely slippery, it has become nigh on impossible for it to be removed by hand, and thus the dog's life is laid on the line. A rubber bone or rubber ring, on which a grasp can be taken, is considerably safer!

For no particular reason, other than for the convenience of writing, I am referring to the dog in its masculine form.

GRASS-SURFACE TRAINING

The initial stages of training a dog to track, whilst under the control of its handler, requires the dog to make use of its natural instinct to chase and catch its prey. As in most dog training exercises, a dog's natural instincts are channelled for the purpose of the handler, and tracking is no exception.

When hunting in the wild, a dog, like all predators, will use a combination of senses, and in particular he will make use of the senses of hearing, sight and smell.

In the open expanse of grassy plains, a predator may well see the movement of potential prey and hunt by sight. As it closes in on a herd, it will often inch its way towards its target in order to shorten the distance, thus considerably lessening the odds of failure, before breaking cover with a sprint. But in the confined environs of a forest then this form of hunting may well be of little use, and so different skills are required.

Although the predator may have identified its target by

sight, it is likely that it will have initially identified it by its scent, whether the scent is hanging in the air or through the disturbance of the ground. The prey may well have itself sensed the approach of a predator and instinctively stood silent, with only its scent being left to betray its presence.

Without going into the complexities of an animal's olfactory abilities, the scents detected can be divided into wind scent and ground scent. Wind scent is when the smell of the animal is carried from its body in the air. Ground scent is when the pressure of the animal's weight disturbs the ground and releases smells from plant and insect life which has been damaged as a result. There may also be remnants of the scent of the animal itself on the vegetation on which it has been in direct contact.

In order to channel these hunt-to-kill instincts for the purpose of tracking a human being, it is advisable to bring a young dog up to have fun and to freely play at 'chase and retrieve' and then 'hold and tug' with a knotted piece of rope, cloth or similar. This will not only satisfy the dog's inherent need to hunt, and therefore keep its senses in fine fettle for when there is the requirement to commence the formal training to track and search, but it will also help build the bond between the dog and the handler so the relationship becomes less of that of the master and the servant and more of that of a team.

To track the scent of a stranger, a dog will need to use the scents which remain on the ground. And so, in order to have a good chance of success, in the early stages of training, it would be advantageous to make use of lush, grassy fields, which have not been used for any purpose during the previous twenty-four hours, or so.

To train a dog to develop the skills which it has inherited from ancestors who have survived by hunting on grassy surfaces, is not too difficult. As far as hard-surface tracking is concerned, with the challenges of there being considerably less scent to detect, then it is probably better to wait until the dog has been successful on grass. For the time being it is important to make it easy for the dog to finish each stage on success, and grass surfaces are ideal for this purpose.

The dog will be required to follow the track, or trail, with the scent of the damaged or disturbed grassy surface. This damage or disturbance having been caused by the weight of the tracklayer's footsteps.

In the very early stages of training if the handler is able to see the signs of the footsteps in the grass then that is not necessarily a disadvantage. After all, the handler can then instantly assess how well the dog is responding to the training. It is, however, important for the handler not to get in the habit of believing that the footsteps seen are those of the tracklayer, as in practical applications it is often not the case. The handler must learn to read and believe the dog and not be swayed by his or her own eyes and assumptions!

There are no set rules as to what age a dog should commence its training, but rather it will be dependent on the maturity and aptitude of the individual. A German Shepherd dog may well respond positively at the age of six months and when the tracking harness fits comfortably. However, it was not until my Rhodesian Ridgeback bitch had reached the age of fifteen months, and when she was sufficiently past that scatty puppy age, that she was mature

TRACK AND SEARCH: A DOG TRAINING GUIDE

enough to respond to the training with the desired interest.

To commence the training, it is advisable to start at the upwind end of the field so that the dog starts to track downwind. This will encourage the dog to keep its nose close to the ground, and so minimize the instinct to try and wind-scent the end-of-track article, thus negating the need to track. If the dog learns that the end-of-track article, the prey, can be located by a means other than from tracking, then he may well develop a habit of hunting for the scent in the air. As a result of this he could be discouraged from tracking altogether.

In the initial stages of track training, the end-of-track article should be familiar to the dog. It should be something that he enjoys playing with and carrying. A rubber bone; a rubber ring or a small child's shoe would be good end-of-track articles in these early stages. These are articles which are likely to be favoured by a dog and therefore worthwhile for him to make the effort to search for. Additionally, they are large enough for the handler to hold on to whilst rewarding the dog by playing tug, once the exercise is finished. If the dog shows no particular interest in articles and is reluctant to do a retrieve, then it may be worthwhile to consider using a length of heavy cloth with knots tied in it, so as to facilitate a grip. Interest can then be regained by playing a rough and tumble game of tug with the article, thus simulating its prey. With the desire to hang on to its prey being encouraged, then it is possible that a more general interest in the finding of articles may be achieved.

As the dog will be working on a harness and a line, I feel it is important at this point to mention a few points about line handling.

As mentioned earlier, the line will be about thirty feet in length and probably made out of a strong but soft material such as sash-window cord. It is normally carried with the majority of it being looped in the left hand. The remaining line is drawn across the front of the handler and held high; that is to say about head height, and in the right hand. Obviously, if the handler is left-handed then this is reversed. This method of line-handling prevents the dog from becoming entangled in the tracking-line and is therefore not distracted from focusing on tracking. The line can be lengthened or shortened by the release or the formation of a single loop at a time. Whilst the dog is working, the line between the dog and handler should be taut, but not to such a degree that it will pull the dog away from its task. As the right hand grasps the line, the handler should be able to feel the slightest variation in its tension and therefore be able to react accordingly. A surge on the line usually indicates that the dog is firmly on the track, and a loosening may well suggest a weakening of, or for that matter, a total loss of the scent. This could be down to either a turn having been made by the tracklayer in trials or a training situation or, if in a real-life practical pursuit, the target has managed to get into a vehicle and thus leave the scene with no more track for the dog to find.

TRACK AND SEARCH: A DOG TRAINING GUIDE

FIRST LESSON

Remembering to be at the upwind end of the field, put a marker post in the ground to indicate the start of the track which is to be laid.

Without making a fuss, slip the harness on the dog and attach the tracking-line to the ring at the top of the harness.

Before reaching the start post, roll the end-of-track article about fifteen to twenty feet along the ground in front of the dog and allow him to chase and catch the article. If the dog shows insufficient interest, then consider bouncing the article through the grass at a height and speed that may give the impression that the article is quickly appearing and disappearing in the grass. This is similar to what is seen when a rabbit is hopping through the grass, and so, hopefully, the dog's hunting instinct will then be aroused. When the he catches, or pounces, on the article, quietly praise him. Do not call him back to you, as in the retrieve, but rather, go to him, shortening the line, hand-over-hand as you approach. Then, gently and without further ado, remove the article from him and hold it in a way that his interest is maintained.

Have an assistant hold the dog whilst it is still in its harness and on the line and then walk towards the start post. When at the start post, turn and face the dog and gain his attention by showing him the article.

Walk away from the dog, downwind, for about fifty yards. Whilst walking away from him, keep his interest by teasing and exciting him with the article; throwing it up in the air, catching it then pretending to place it on the ground.

After about fifty yards, turn and face the dog, making it obvious to him that the article has been placed on the ground and left. Scuff the grass before laying the article as it will give extra scent for the dog to focus on. The dog should be thinking of this article as being his prey or property, and so he should have the desire to seize it for himself. On this first occasion the article should still be visible to the dog from the start post. Return to the dog along the same track as was walked outwards, scuffing the grass surface with each step. If the dog is excited and raring to go, then there is a good chance of a successful outcome.

Without saying anything and so as not to distract the dog, take the line from the assistant and allow the dog to go for the article. As the article will be visible, the dog will, no doubt, rely on the sense of sight to regain possession of his prey or property. This is not a problem on this first occasion as it is important for the dog to have success in each stage of this early training. Whilst the dog is rushing forwards to find the article, the handler should be careful not to allow the dog to have too much line, nor should the handler risk distraction by jerking on the line. It is also important for the handler to walk, albeit at a brisk pace, and not to run and thus lose control.

When the dog reaches and picks up the article, then the dog should be praised and the article taken. Then, as a reward, and as a sign that the exercise has ended, it can be thrown a few yards for the dog to chase and *kill*.

Whilst this is being done, the assistant should collect the pole and reposition it some thirty feet beyond the point where the end-of-track article was found; thus, a fresh track can be laid in an area which is still unused, having not already been walked on.

STEP-BY-STEP DIAGRAMMATIC GUIDE

The diagrams which have been used in the text which follow have each been taken from the author's previous publication of 1988: A GUIDE TO TRACKING AND THE SQUARE SEARCH.

The solid line in the diagrams signify the section which is to be worked by the dog and handler team.

The flag pole at one end indicating the start, and the dot at the other indicating the end-of-track article.

The broken line signifies the direction which the tracklayer takes after laying the track, and it is not part of the track to be worked.

The three parallel arrows signify the direction of the wind, or breeze, and not its strength.

TRACK AND SEARCH: A DOG TRAINING GUIDE

Step 1

Single-leg track, with an article left on the ground to indicate the end of the track. The tracklayer has walked back along the original line of the track, therefore doubling up on the amount of scent for the dog to follow.

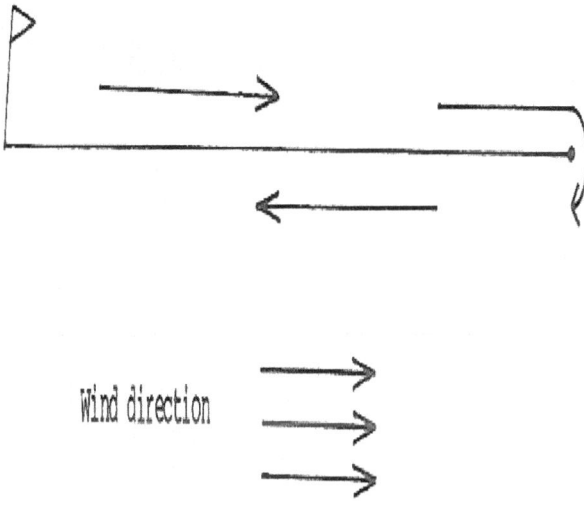

Step 2

Single-leg track laid with an end-of-track article.

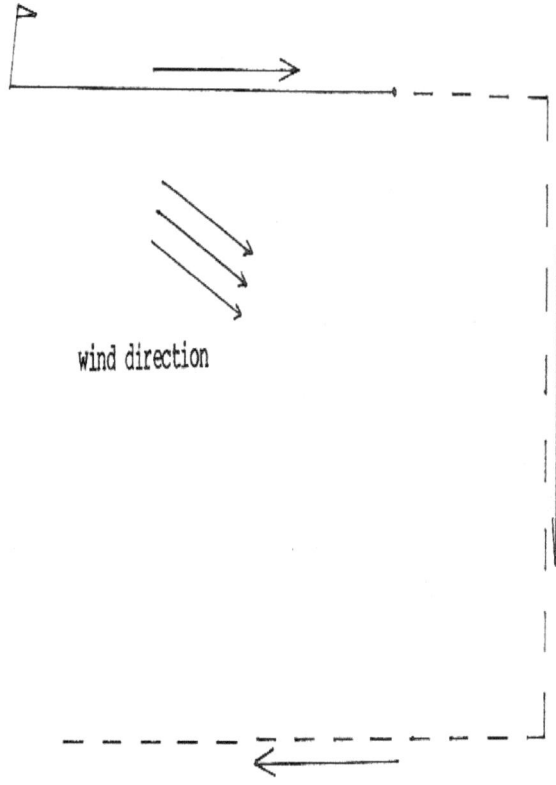

It should be noted that the tracklayer has, for several yards, continued to walk in the same direction of the actual track before returning to the start via a different route.

This means that the dog will not associate a turn with the end-of-track article. It will also ensure that the track has the normal amount of scent for the dog to follow. In order not to confuse him with the scent from the track-layer's return route drifting across the actual track, it would be helpful if the turn on the return journey is negotiated downwind.

Step 3

Introduction of a turn to the track.

The final leg of the track is laid downwind. Again, it will be seen that the tracklayer has continued in the same direction as the track for several yards prior to making his or her way back to the start.

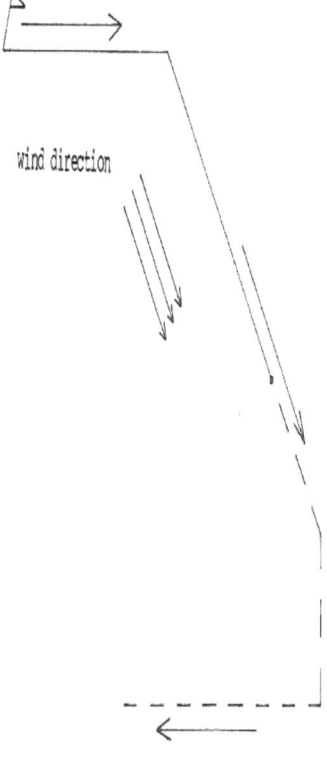

Step 4

Introduction of a second turn. Depending on the dog's progress, leave the track to mature for around fifteen minutes before allowing the dog to run it. At this early stage, each leg of the track should be about seventy-five yards in length.

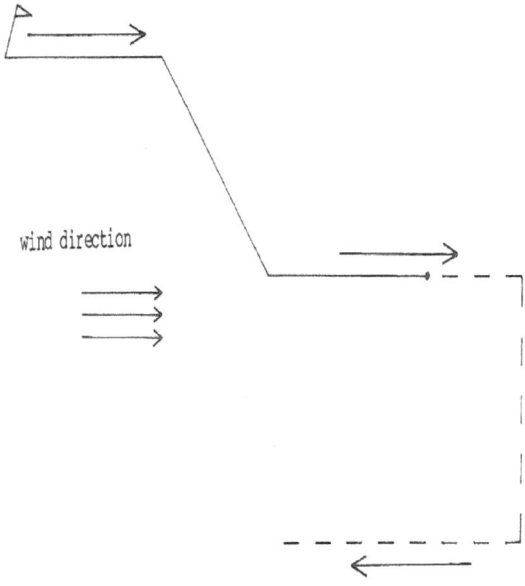

Step 5

Alternative introduction to a second turn. Again, depending on the dog's progress, leave the track to mature for around fifteen minutes, with each leg of the track being about seventy-five yards in length.

TRACK AND SEARCH: A DOG TRAINING GUIDE

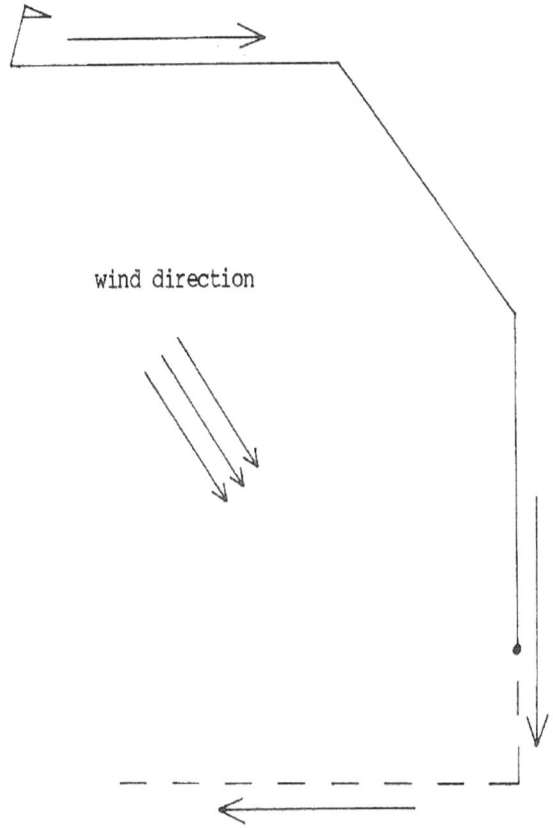

Step 6

This track pattern introduces a right-angled turn. It also starts off with the dog getting used to tracking *into* the wind, and not *with* the wind as before. However, to encourage the dog to associate success with following the trail of the tracklayer's footsteps, and not searching for the scent of the end-of-track article in the air, the final leg has been laid downwind.

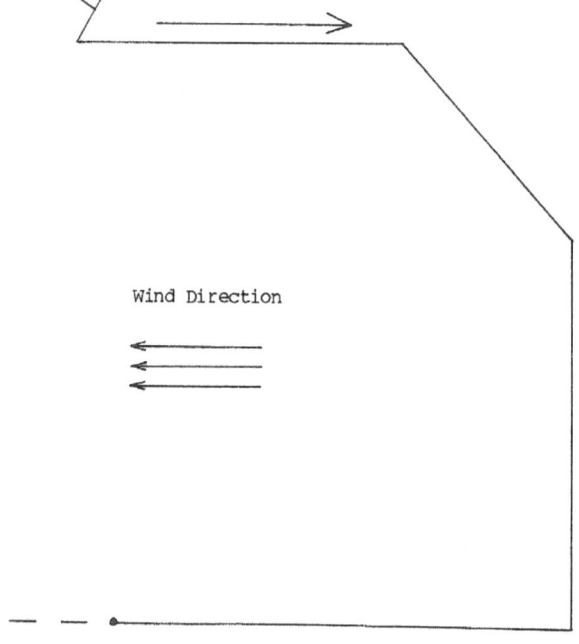

TRACK AND SEARCH: A DOG TRAINING GUIDE

Step 7

This track pattern introduces an acute-angle turn. It is laid so as to include turns to both the left and the right. When a dog has reached this stage, the track should be run with around a 20 to 30 minute time-lapse between it having been laid and it being commenced.

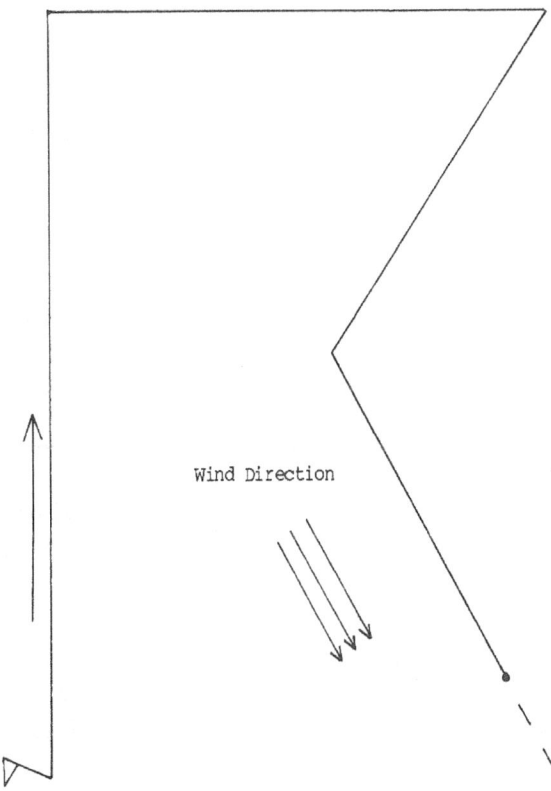

Step 8

The following track patterns are typical of those which are laid in the Utility Dog stake of a British Working Trial.

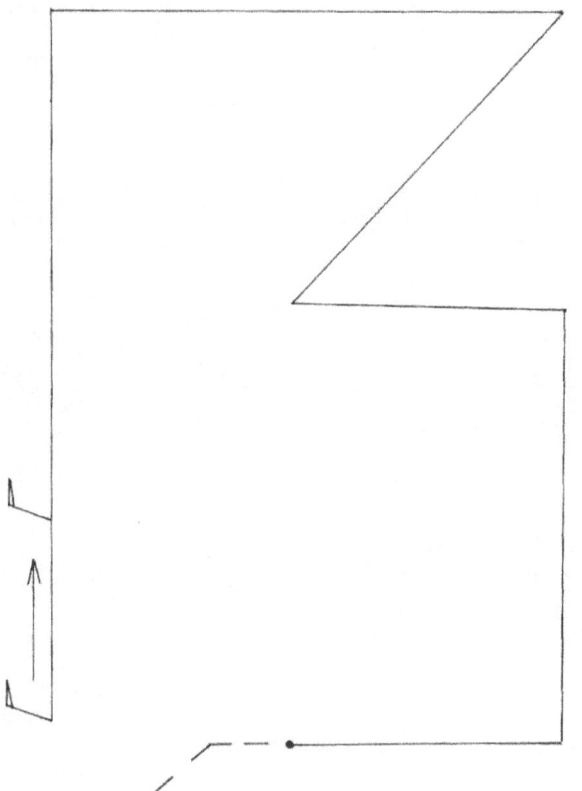

TRACK AND SEARCH: A DOG TRAINING GUIDE

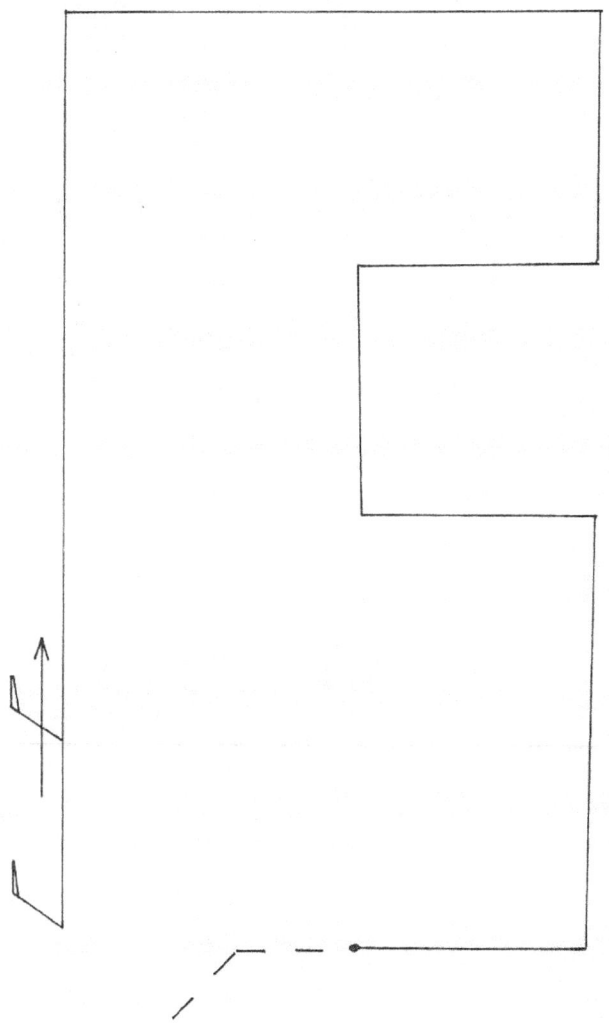

The tracks will be around 800 yards in length, with two articles; the second being left somewhere along the track and at the tracklayer's discretion.

They track will have been laid at least 30 minutes prior to the track being run.

There will be a start pole at the beginning of the track, with a second pole placed about 30 yards further along the track. This indicates not only the start of the track, but also the initial direction of travel of the tracklayer.

When a dog has reached the standard required to compete in Working Trials competitions, then neither the wind direction, nor the lushness of the grass will be taken into consideration by the tracklayer. After all, the trials are designed to test the dog and handler's ability to track a missing or absconding person, whose identity may not necessarily be known.

In the more advanced stakes there will be single post to indicate the start of the track, and the time lapse between the laying of the track and the running of the track will be increased to 1½ hours for both the Working Dog and Patrol Dog stakes.

These stakes will also have two articles for the dog to locate somewhere between the start and the finish of the track. In the Tracking Dog stake there is a third article to be found, and the time-lapse between the laying of the track and its running is increased to that of a period of 3 hours.

In U.K. Working Trials marks are awarded for each exercise and are apportioned as follows:

Utility Dog stake: Track @ 90 marks: Two articles @ 10 marks each.

Working Dog stake: Track @ 90 marks: Two articles @ 10 marks each.

Tracking Dog stake: Track @ 100 marks: Three articles @ 10 marks each.

Patrol Dog stake: Track @ 60 marks: Two articles @ 10 marks each.

HARD-SURFACE TRACKING

When a dog has proved to be competent at tracking on grass, then it may be required, for practical purposes, to train on hard surfaces. For example: roads; car parks; pedestrian precincts and industrial estates. Civilian working trials do not cater for hard-surface tracking.

The main problem with a hard surface is that there is little to no vegetation being damaged by the weight of a person's footsteps. Therefore, there is considerably less scent for a dog to detect and then follow. It is likely that the dog will be limited to scenting the traces of footwear and any damage sustained by minor vegetation and insects on the ground.

The training system for hard surfaces is, in essence, the same as that for grass surfaces.

In the early stages, and in order to give the dog more scent to work on, it may be useful to choose a broken hard surface area where patches of vegetation have forced their way through.

If this is not readily available then the tracklayer should exaggerate the scent by scuffing the soles of the shoes in nearby vegetation, and then scuff them again while laying the first leg of the track. This will allow more scent to adhere to the surface.

Tracking from a grass surface to a hard surface, and then back again, may also introduce the dog to the hard-surface tracking experience; so long as the track is not left to mature for too long. An example of this would be for the track to be laid so that it crosses a road or a small car park.

The advantage to this method is that as the dog will already be tracking when the hard surface is reached, then the sudden reduction in scent will not deter it too much.

Once back on the grass surface, the dog will reconnect with the track with ease, and so locate the end-of-track article and finish the exercise on success.

The progression of track patterns should be as previously described in the grass-surface training section.

If the dog can successfully negotiate hard-surface tracks which have matured for twenty minutes, then this should be considered as being quite acceptable.

To mark the start of a hard-surface track, a traffic cone or a post with a flat base may be used.

If the dog will not keep its nose to the ground, then consider placing an article on each track leg. This should help the dog to maintain interest in the exercise.

The handler should keep the tracking-line a little shorter than when handling on a grass surface.

LAYING TRACKS

Before starting to lay the track, take a look at the area available and make a rough plan of the proposed track, with a view to including turns of different angles and directions. Tracklayers should ensure that the end of the track is such that they do not find that their exit is not possible without fouling the previously laid track.

Position the start pole and make a note of the time. The age of the track is determined from this moment to when the dog commences the exercise.

Each leg of the track should be straight; although it has been known for curves to be used in the pattern of tracks in advanced stakes.

In order to ensure that a straight line is walked, then it is advisable for the tracklayer to line-up on two landmarks. For example, the roof of a building in the distance may appear to be immediately above a gap in the hedge, and so, by keeping these two markers lined up with each other while walking towards them, the line should remain relatively straight. This will also serve to put the dog back on track if, for some reason, the trail has been lost.

The length of each leg of a track can also be measured by noting the number of paces.

When it comes to making a turn, it is important to be able to remember the exact point of the turn. Again, the reason being to enable the dog to be put right if necessary.

There are two common methods which are often combined.

The first is to use a natural marker on the ground, such as a bare patch of earth; a clump of weeds; an unusual rock, or anything else which may stand out. There is no need to turn on the exact spot of the natural marker but rather a metre or so before or after it.

The second method is to make use of the same system as mentioned earlier with regard to lining up on distant landmarks. When approaching a suitable point to make a turn, then look out for two more landmarks in the direction in which the turn is to be made. The point where the imaginary line of the new leg of the track intersects with the imaginary line of the already laid track is fixed.

Subsequent legs of the track can be lined up in the same way. If it is possible that due to adverse weather conditions, or failing light, that the distant landmarks may become obscured, then it is worth using landmarks which are not too distant.

This method of lining up two imaginary lines set with fixed points can also be used when positioning mid-track articles.

Some tracklayers make a note on a pad of the track pattern, including distances, markers and positions of articles.

A good tracklayer should easily be able to put a dog and handler back on to the track in the unlikely event of there being a loss of way. If this cannot be achieved then a novice dog may become disheartened and consequently be put off from doing the exercise.

TRACK AND SEARCH: A DOG TRAINING GUIDE

There is an interesting exercise which can be used to test the ability of a tracklayer.

I can recall how, during my initial training, I was asked to lay a track for an experienced dog across some wild and rugged terrain, leaving six small articles en-route. An hour later, and when the time had come for the dog to run the track, my instructor told me that the dog would not be doing it after all. I was to retrace my steps and recover each of the articles personally. It was far from easy. As a result, I learnt that if the dog had lost the track, and I had been required to put it right, then I would have struggled.

The role of the tracklayer is extremely important when training a dog for this discipline and, what is more, it can only improve with experience.

THE SQUARE SEARCH

The purpose of this exercise is for the dog to locate and retrieve four articles, each of which possess the scent of a stranger, from an area of twenty-five yards square. The handler may not enter the square during the exercise, and so must work the dog from the outside. There are five minutes, timed from the moment the dog enters the square, for the dog and handler team to complete the exercise.

This exercise requires four marker posts, to indicate each corner of the square, and a selection of articles for the dog to locate. These search articles should include a variety of materials. For example: metal; plastic; card; cork; wood; rubber; leather and cloth. In fact, they can be made of any material, so long as it's in such a way that they would not be injurious to the dog. The size of the articles should range from around four, or five, inches in length; i.e. a short piece of garden hose, down to something the size of a shotgun cartridge case. The larger articles are to be used in the initial stages of training to enable the dog to be certain to finish on success.

When laying each article in the square area it is important to remember exactly where it was left. On completion of any training session all articles must be recovered, as an article left on the ground could cause injury, or even death, to livestock. Although less likely, it could also cause damage to farm machinery.

SQUARE SEARCH TRAINING

As in tracking, the natural instinct for a dog to hunt for prey is channelled into serving the purpose of the handler. For evidential purposes it is important for the dog to recover any articles undamaged, and so it would be useful if the dog had already been taught to retrieve and to readily return a dumbbell to the handler. In a working trial scenario the article is expected to be taken out of the square area by the dog, but a perfect return to the handler, as in a formal retrieve, is not essential.

Before embarking on the structured search training, it may be worthwhile getting in the habit of carrying a pocketful of articles when out on a walk. Without nagging the dog, toss the articles into some long grass and, in play, encourage it to find them. Once an article is located, praise the dog and encourage him to bring the article to you. This exercise should not be a chore for the dog, with the insistence of a perfect textbook retrieve; rather, it should be a time for enjoyment.

When throwing the article for the dog, hold the article in

your hand and blow on it. Not only will this add some more scent, but it will also attract the dog's attention. It should not take too long for the dog to associate the handler *blowing in the hand* with the game of searching for articles. If the dog starts to search and loses his impetus, then words of encouragement (the tone of voice is what gives the encouragement), along with a *blowing in the hand*, will usually get the dog to resume the search with added zest.

It must be remembered that even in the *play* mode, this is a team effort and there is no room for the handler to cause distraction or to try to assert his or her dominance. The dog must be watched carefully while it is searching, in order for the handler to learn how to recognize when the dog has picked up the scent of an article. If there is an indication from the dog that an article has been sensed, then it may not hurt to add a little encouragement for the dog to home-in on it.

Once the dog has demonstrated sufficient success in the *play* setting, then structured training can begin. Of course, most dogs do not need much encouragement as they will happily enter the formal training schedule without a problem.

To commence the structured training, it may be advisable to use a field which has not been recently walked on by others or fouled by other dogs. That way the dog will not be distracted by too many other scents.

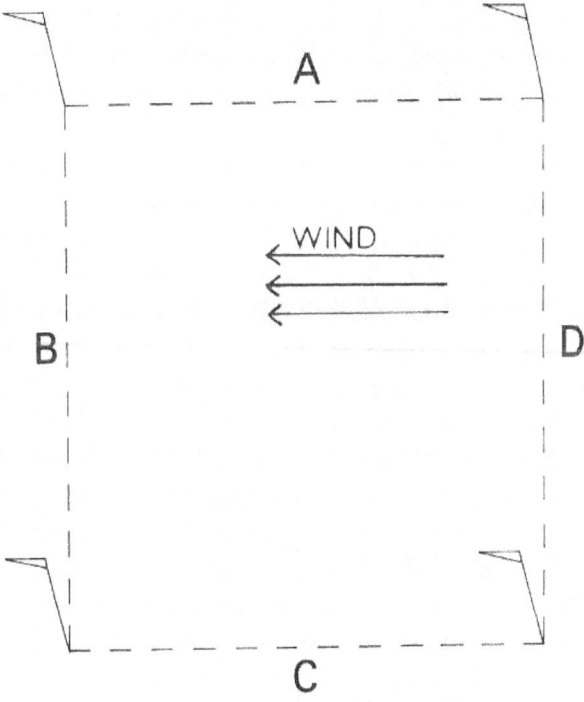

Mark out a square area of around fifteen yards each side with a marker post at each corner. If possible, position the square so that the wind enters a side at right-angles, as shown in the diagram.

The handler should be positioned outside the square, in the middle of side B, with an assistant holding the dog on a leash. The handler should show the dog the article, which should be around five or six inches long and fun for the dog to play with. A length of leather, or a possibly a young child's leather shoe, would be ideal. Walk backwards into the square, while maintaining the dog's interest at all times. Scuff the ground with a foot and lay the article on the scuff mark. Once done, return to the dog and send him into the square, having given him the blow-in-the-hand signal, as mentioned earlier. When the article is located, the dog should be encouraged to carry it out of the square area and towards the handler. If this stage is successful, then, after giving the dog praise, the next stage can be commenced using the same square area.

Position the dog, as before, at side B. The handler should

take three or four articles into the square and allow the dog to watch them being placed. Before, after and in-between the placing of the articles, the handler should also pretend to place additional articles on the ground so that when the dog commences the search it does not rely on memory but uses its sense of smell instead. Again, when the articles have been placed, the handler should return to the dog and, on command, recommence a search.

The dog will often make a beeline to the place where the handler was either first or last seen to pretend to leave an article. When the dog reaches this point and discovers that the article is not there, he will naturally resort to searching.

If the dog searches unaided, the handler should not distract him from the task, but should remain silent. If, however, the dog starts to struggle, then some encouragement by voice and hand movements will be required. When an article is found, the handler should always encourage the dog to carry the article out of the square as if doing a retrieve.

Once one article is recovered, then the dog can be sent in

for a second. Do not be tempted to push for a third and a fourth at this stage as the dog could become bored. Additionally, the chances of a successful outcome are greatly reduced as the number of articles decrease, and so, as I stress throughout, always try and finish on success.

If the structured training seems to be too much for the dog, then it is possible that it was commenced prematurely. Never be afraid to go back to basics and return to *play* mode.

The next stage is for the articles to be laid while the dog is out of sight. The method of search will be the same as described above; again, not insisting on all of the available articles being retrieved.

If the dog readily demonstrates success in the exercise, then it is time to commence searching from either side A or side C. That is to say, across the square, yet still downwind of some of the articles. This will educate the hander in *reading* the dog and recognizing when it wind-scents an article before homing-in on it. The dog's general expression and pose will change when picking up the scent of an article.

Early recognition of these indications will make for better teamwork later, especially when the articles are smaller and therefore not readily visible to the handler. This is also the stage when the articles should be laid by another person so that the dog does not look solely for the scent of its handler.

As the dog progresses, then the square area should be increased to the full twenty-five yards each side, with the articles being reduced in size and left to settle in the square for some ten minutes or so. The person who lays the articles should also walk all over the square area, so as to reduce the likelihood of the dog *tracking* to an article. After all, this exercise is designed to test the dog's ability to locate property by scent.

Remembering that the allocated time for the exercise is five minutes from the moment the dog enters the square, then it is possible to make use of the unmonitored time. When approaching the square, it is advisable to approach from the downwind edge and walk the length of the side, while observing the dog's reaction and seeing if any articles are readily visible. The dog may even be seen to pick up the wind-scent of an article prior to actually entering the square, and the starting of the clock.

There are several methods of working a square. One method is to allow the dog to work the whole square until he has difficulty in locating an article. The handler can then get the dog to work the square systematically, and in quarters. The handler should not remain static but should move around the edge of the square, thus shortening the distance required for the dog to carry the articles out of the square. The shorter the distance, the less chance of an article being dropped within the bounds of the square. If possible, the handler should avoid walking, or standing, upwind of the search area as the scent could mask that of any remaining articles.

Another method is to work the dog to-and-fro across the square between sides A and C, gradually working into the wind from side B, up to side D.

When all of the articles have been located, and then carried by the dog out of the square area, they should be presented to the judge by the handler before the dog is allowed to relax and play. Of course, in a training session the reward of play is almost instant.

PRACTICAL APPLICATION

The search method described in the previous sections can be used practically for searching for both stolen and lost property.

A search may be in a relatively small or otherwise restricted area; for example, a country path.

In this scenario the dog can be worked into the wind, and across the path from edge to edge. If appropriate, he can be directed into any recesses.

If the area to be searched is large, for example, a playing field or on open moors, then the four poles can be used to systematically mark out squares, as in working trials. Again, in order to take advantage of any wind, the first squares should be positioned at the furthest point downwind. If the first square has been worked without success, then the square can be repositioned by moving two poles across so as to form a new square which is butted up against the first square, and so on. A whole field can be covered with this method of sectioning it into individual search areas.

It should be remembered that in the case of a dog being used to try and locate an item which is of high value, fragile or possibly of forensic interest for fingerprinting or DNA analysis, the handler should watch the dog for any indication, and, if possible, retrieve the item before it is picked up and mouthed. In this case, the play item, which should always be readily available, should be immediately substituted as a reward. At this stage, and for the information of those of my police officer colleagues who had sometimes asked me the question, I can confirm that this is the only reason that my truncheon came to be peppered in teeth marks!

If in doubt, then always trust your dog

TRACK AND SEARCH: A DOG TRAINING GUIDE

THE AUTHOR

Born in Devon, the author spent his formative years in Northern Rhodesia, now Zambia, before returning to Devon at the age of seven.

In addition to performing a variety of roles within the police service, he has previously served as a dog handler in West Cornwall.

Following his retirement from the police he has worked in Patient Transport before re-locating from the south-west of England to County Donegal, Ireland and then to Pembrokeshire, in south-west Wales, before returning to re-settle in the south-west of England

www.ingramcontent.com/pod-product-compliance
Lightning Source LLC
Chambersburg PA
CBHW031427040426
42444CB00006B/723